THE SUN
HAS FORGOTTEN
WHERE I LIVE

The Sun
Has Forgotten
Where I Live

Poems

Christian McPherson

CANADA

Library and Archives Canada Cataloguing in Publication

McPherson, Christian
The sun has forgotten where I live : poems / Christian McPherson.

ISBN 978-1-926942-00-1

I. Title.

PS8625.P53S86 2011   C811'.6   C2010-908068-8

Printed and bound in Canada on 100% recycled paper.

Now Or Never Publishing
#704, 1460 Barclay Street
Vancouver, British Columbia
Canada V6G 1J5

nonpublishing.com
Fighting Words.

For Marty, Molly, Henry, and Buddy
who always bring the sun with them

Contents

LANDING

I love the sound
of jets landing

when I was a kid
my father and I
would drive out to the airport
and park by the fence
and watch the planes
land

they were so loud
I could feel their weight
in my bones
when they roared by

there was something about
sitting in that station wagon
like going to church
like going to confession

as an adult I have a house
located on a flight path

sometimes I lie in bed
waiting for the sounds
of planes landing
sometimes I lie in bed
waiting for forgiveness.

An Explanation

I woke up on the ceiling
gravity had let me down

I was afraid to go outside
I might have floated up
like a helium balloon

but then gravity
showed up
late
while I was in the bathroom

that's how I cut myself shaving
that's why I'm late

she said "It's not cute after a while."

APOLOGIES TO DAD

So when I write
something personal down
from my childhood
like the day
my father
walked out on my mother
and gave me
a 20 dollar bill
like it would make it
alright
       (throw money at the problem)

do I write for catharsis?
do I write to entertain you?
or do I write
to discredit my father
to discredit myself?

heck, you don't even know
if I'm telling you
the truth

maybe that never happened?
maybe somebody will pay me
20 bucks for this poem?

whatever the case may be
I'll have to live
with myself.

MARK MY WORDS

Scratch them with a penny
        on the cell wall
                of the broken dream prison

smudge them with lipstick
        on the bathroom mirror
           of the dead movie star

draw them with crayons
        on the sketchpad
                provided by the psychiatrist

paint them with blood
        on the inside
           of Egyptian tombs

carve them with the butterfly knife
        deep into the flesh
           of the lover's tree

tattoo them with the buzzing needle
        on the skin of the circus freak
                under the nomad big top

brand them with the rubber stamp
        on the cereal box
           of an instant life

vomit them with the orange finger
        alphagetti on the white bowl
           of the toilet

mark them with the quivering pen
    in the little black book
        you keep under your bed.

MUSICAL BEDS

Woke up
clutching my two and a half
       year old daughter's stuffed bear
       she was on the other side
       of our queen bed
       cuddling a Dora doll

dashed quickly
       to the bathroom
              and pissed away
              my morning erection
              before she woke up
              and asked
              "Daddy, what's in your underwear?"

stealthily slipped back under the duvet
       I could smell my wife's hair
       on the pillow

we had made love
here
and had been drifting off
when my son's tooth
showed up
and the whole family
was embroiled in a game
of musical beds

I fell back asleep
       and dreamt of migrating crows

woke up again
       this time my daughter's face
       is an inch from mine

she whispers
       "Hi daddy, I want some juice."

BUBBLES

Standing on the edge of the bridge
my day job like concrete shoes
nudged by the fat man
       with the diet soda

freefalling

hitting the water

air leaves my lungs

I watch the bubbles

reflections of
            mortgage payments
        grilled cheese sandwiches
          the banality of TV

       float silvery up

down
        I land in the seabed batter
           of the gooey bottom

I hold my breath
clutching the lotto life preserver   ticket
and wish I wasn't an atheist.

CURSE OF THE HAPPY WITCH

I went to say
goodnight
to my daughter
and she was upside down
in the bed
feet on her pillow

I sat down
on the edge
and looked at her feet
then I grabbed them
"Oh Molly! Oh no!" I cried
as I gently shook them
"A witch came and turned your head
into feet!"
"Daddy," said a happy voice
"Yes," I said to the feet
"Daddy," she repeated
"Molly, that was a nasty witch
        to turn your head into feet!"
"Daddy," she repeated
I looked down to smiley teeth
"Oh, phew, I thought a witch
had turned your head into feet!
Thank goodness you're ok!"

"Daddy," she said, "do it again."

and with that I was cursed
to do it over and over
and over again.

INJURY

I knew a woman
who used to walk
with a fruit salad bounce
in her step
and spoke daisies of her daughter
her life blood

when you hurt your arm
people tend to favour it
coddle it
protect it from further injury

one day she told me
that her daughter was
going to move out
and move in
with a boy

then she carried herself
like her whole body was sprained

I thought
one day
I'll be injured
like that
too.

Little Circular Mirror

I went
to the dentist
the other day

read movie reviews
from last month's
Maclean's

finally I was called
in

I lay back
in the chair
and looked up
at the ceiling

it was covered
with cutesy
little posters
of sunsets
and rainbows

one read:
       "A happy memory
             is a joy forever."

I asked the dental
hygienist if the corollary
to this was:
       "A sad memory
             is a torment forever."

she didn't seem amused
she said, "I certainly hope not."
then she poked me
in the gums
with a sharp instrument
and made me bleed.

Magic

I chugged down
my last beer
really fast
   turns out
   there was a genie
   in the bottle

I burped up a wish

when I went back
to the fridge
there was
a six pack
sitting
there
behind
the expired
mayonnaise.

THE BEAT

Trying to beat
the lunch rush
to the psychiatrist's
couch

trying to beat
to the tune
of a different
drummer

trying to beat
the lumpy parts
smooth

trying to beat
every last inch
out of
a cliché

trying to beat
it out on the page

trying to beat
the devil
at his own
golf game

trying to beat
the odds
even

trying to beat
myself off
to yesterday's porn

trying to beat
the hands of time
but that old reaper
well he just throws me
his sly smile

I give him the finger.

THE DAILY MIGRATION OF THE CROWS

A Hitchcockian dreamscape
it peppers my sky
this flying connect-the-dots puzzle
        thousands of crows
        flying home
        to the wooded area
        behind my house

I see them everyday
on my walk
to
and
from
work

        back
        and
        forth
        my companions
        fly

I love them
like my own children
        who are
        the only reason
        why I'm still
        walking to
            and
            from
            work

do the crows fly out of love
                or necessity
                        or is it
                                the same thing?

Lucky S.O.B.

All I know
is that I love
watching you sleep
your mess of dark hair
a web of angel hair pasta
sliding off the pillow

I think that some lucky S.O.B.
gets to wake up
to you
every day

I think about all the men
who have rubbed themselves
raw
thinking
of you

a very long time ago
I was one of them

and now when I get up
and make you breakfast
just know I do it
not because I love
making breakfast
(although maybe I do)
but because I know
that I am
that lucky son of a bitch.

THE DRAGON

One beer leads to
      one too many
      next thing
      I'm on the lawn
          doing karate moves
              Bruce Lee would be proud
              dragon
                  seeks
                     monkey
              (never even took one lesson)

the dragon
reared its ugly head
again
on the cab ride home

found myself sleeping on the basement floor
(who wants to sleep with a dragon
      his snore is like rattling armor)

woke up
      freezing
screaming
      "Where are the fucking blankets?!"

woke up
      much later
mumbling
      "Where is the Tylenol?"

spent the next two days hungover
      spent the next two weeks with my tail
         between my legs.

The Race to Nowhere

On my elliptical
in my basement
surrounded by
recycling boxes
Halloween decorations
beer empties
laundry
I pump away
fighting the middle-age
bulge

I think of my father
at my age now
fatter than me
really starting to
put it on

and I imagine
him there
with his curly perm
and white undershirt
and blue shorts
on his
'70s stationary
bike

and we start
to race

dad's legs
flying around
like an eggbeater
in batter

me
looking like
a cross-country
ski maniac

we go hard

dad's face turns red
as he stands up
on the pedals
leaning over
the handlebars

he throws me
a smile
that says
he is winning

I push harder
dripping sweat
legs on fire

his legs are a blur

my heart is beating out of my chest

then   BEEP
                    BEEP
BEEP
         BEEP
                    BEEP

my machine tells me
it's over
I'm done
I burned my 800 calories

dad sits back down
and puts his arms up
in victory

my legs slow
to a stop

dad laughs
and fades
away
and I think
maybe I'll live
a little longer
than he did.

My Father's Autopsy

When the cop asked me
"What do you think he died from?"
I took a guess, replying "Maybe a heart attack."
he told me that an autopsy
would be performed

I think of my father
naked
splayed open on a table
like a grade 9 science frog
ribs flowering out
and the coroner is
pulling out his guts
pulling out 8-tracks
of Elvis and The Beach Boys
pulling out a gravy soaked spleen
pulling out a pack of Export A Green king size
pulling out a wedding ring with two electrical burns
pulling out a crucifix stained heart
pulling out hundreds of feet of picture wire
and finally pulling out
the giant tumour on his pancreas
the one that stopped blood flowing to his lungs
the one that killed him

I sew up this memory
and search my imagination for a can of gas
and a match
and light it
cremating the whole thing.

TROUBLES

I sat at a bar with
a man who had one eye
who told me about
how he had lost the other:
       childhood
bows and arrows
       "It's all fun and games
         until someone loses . . ."
his sobriety

he told me about
how he'd lost his wife to cancer
and how he'd lost his job to restructuring
and how he'd lost his soul to the casino
and how he'd lost his heart to go on

he told me about
how his budgie had turned to smack
and how his cake didn't rise
and how his kids were full of hate
and how his car was empty of gas

he told me about
drafty rooms
and curdled milk
and sad dripping sinks
and almost winning the lottery

he told me about
how he ate only tuna and rats for 3 months
and how he didn't shower for 6 days
and how he was in a coma for 9 hours
and how his mother loved him for only 12 minutes

then he told me about
how he had found Jesus
and I told him
I had to go

I never went
to that bar
again.

A Letter to the Mayor

Every day they scream
    when they jump
        off the tall office buildings
            downtown

A
A
A
A
A
A
A
A
A
A
A
A
A
A
A
A
A
H
H
H
H
H

S P L A T !

the city
should really
provide
earplugs.

Lemon Drop

"What the FUCK IS GOING ON?! IS SHE OK?!"

My wife is screaming
from down the hall
she doesn't want to see
what is happening

just last week
we had friends over
and they had their
one year old little girl
with them

all the kids were playing
when the little girl
suddenly went bug-eyed

the mother asked
"What does she have in her mouth?"

nobody answered
        we all just looked at the baby

then the mother screamed
        "WHAT THE FUCK IS IN HER MOUTH?!"

her lacquered red fingernail
scooped the inside of the tiny mouth
like she was digging out an avocado
she found a few teeth
        and nothing else

the baby cried
the mother issued a series of apologies
        "I'm so sorry, I thought she was . . ."

"CHRIS, WHAT'S GOING ON!" screams my wife
still down the hall

I flash back to the room where I spent two days
taking First Aid
I remember DON'T hit them on the back
I remember something about not performing
the Heimlich Manoeuvre on kids
my four year old daughter
is standing before me
eyes like gumballs
mouth open
her hand clutching
the base of her little neck
silent

I don't know where
my daughter got the idea
either TV or a movie
but she had been asking me
for a lemon drop candy
"Pleeeeeeeeease can I have one
        please please please"

I bought a small tin of lemon drop candies
and now here I am
neurons painting images
of brain damage
of ambulances
of funerals

"DO I NEED TO CALL 911?"

good question

I grab my daughter
around the waist
and pick her up
and POP
the lemon drop flies
and TICK TICKED across the floor

then after the tears
and the calming down
I throw those little yellow
fuckers
in the trash.

First Sign of Autumn

Looked like God
dribbled red paint
on a tree
near my cottage

I spit in disgust
knowing soon
he would whitewash
the whole
canvas.

A QUICK FUCK

I was riding my bike
to work
and a beautiful woman
was jogging
the other way

our gazes locked
like we were fucking
just for a second

then she was gone.

GARBAGE DAY

The clouds kissed the ground
and I had to walk to work
in a soupy horror-movie fog

as I passed by a church
I noticed
all the bags of trash
by the side of the road

I had a vision of the priest
down there
in the basement
of that church
wearing one of those
butcher's aprons
holding a chainsaw

there is blue smoke
and screaming
and tons and tons
of blood
as the priest
cuts the devil
into little bits

when the priest is done
he cleans up
and he stuffs
arms
       legs
               pointy tail
      etc.
into plastic
garbage bags
and drags them
outside to the curb

looked just like
normal trash

it was
only three weeks
until Halloween.

GLOSSY ADVERTISING

4 page layout in a magazine:

the torso of a voluptuous woman
with pale creamy skin
clutching an electrifying green
bushel of broccoli to her bare bosom

crucified Christ on the cross
clutching in each hand
like this was his true burden
blood dripping broccoli

a young freckled Irish girl
hair as red as a strawberry
licking as if it were a lollipop
a contrasting clump of broccoli

and a cocksure cowboy
riding a calico horse
with gorgeous leather boots
having broccoli for spurs

what a clever way to sell blue jeans.

Life Plan for Recovering Addicts
(and most everyone else)

Get off the crystal-meth layaway package
and get on the three-storey tinfoil dildo
Happymeal plan

buy all the fucking nonsense
until your skeleton pops
out of its skin
and jogs
to the corner store
and picks up
a litre of milk
a loaf of brown bread
and 20 bucks in lotto tickets

show up to work on time
and punch a clock-sucker
in the face

drink whiskey until you fall asleep

repeat until death

the end.

I Give You the World

I give you
the machete genocides
the twisted sex offenders
the surprise brain tumours

I give you
the infected cut
the shirking of responsibility
the nuclear weapons

I give you
the tortures
the prisons
the executions

I give you
religion
farts
vomit

I give you all of this
       I give you the World

but I also give you
the disco ball
the chocolate cake
the fruit salad

I also give you
the winning goal
the creative spirit
the artist's paintbrush

I also give you
the hot coffee
the spa
the mountain air

I also give you
John Coltrane
Mathematics
Love

It was all given to me
in pretty much
the same
shape
as I
give it to you
now

do the best
you can
with it

then
pass
it on.

Buddhist Jet Lag

I was living
in the now
but then I fell
a few seconds behind

I would just miss
the elevator
the bus

and before I knew it
I was living
in the 30-minutes-ago

I would
burn my rice
be late for work

then things got worse
I started living
in the two-hours-ago

I was missing
doctors' appointments
lunch dates

it crept up on me
and all of a sudden
I was living
in yesterday

I sang Beatles songs
and got fired from work

I became depressed
hit the bottle
ended up living
in the past
babbling on my couch
about the good ole days

then came the intervention
people said "you can't live in the past"
people said "you need to think about the future"
the men in white coats came
as did the pills
the rubber rooms
the drooling

now I'm all better
now I'm back in the now
now I might actually be a few seconds ahead

I catch things before they fall
people think I'm just moving things around
but I know the future
because I live there.

Reality Check

Waking up after
the mad scientists
have been sneaking around
in the dead of the night
swapping brains

the neuropathways
are all mixed up
and now the wood
in the sculptor's hand
(which use to be the butcher's)
feels like meat
and she ends up
carving a headless chicken

the butcher stacks
hamburger balls
like snowmen
and makes a garden display
out of ribs and chops

the doctor can't find
the pulse on the piano
and the musician
hears a song
in every heartbeat

I lie in bed
and wonder
if my memories
have been implanted

am I just a brain in a vat?
does it matter anyway?

I get up
get dressed
and to my surprise
my hands remember
how to operate
the toaster.

Canadian Psycho

Waiting opportunity
fulfilling struggle
latex gloved lunacy
and a black black muzzle

breath of formaldehyde
bony cold fingers
a coward in style
in shadows you linger

robbed your mother's tears
stole your wife's humour
blamed your father's eyes
and denied all the rumours

inverted responsibility
for a bottle drowned
sought credibility
wearing a blaming frown

love of others
is to see fault in them
if others hate you
everyone you condemn

a piece of work
a testament to humanity
dark creativity lurks
behind eyes of insanity.

Sick Bastard

There is a man
driving around my neighbourhood
in a white van
(why are they always white?)
he doesn't have the golden 'AN'
but maybe something just as alluring
as Sesame Street
     a lost puppy
     "Will you hop in and help me find him?"

what would I do if he came to my house?
would I calmly call 911?
would I make sure he gets the help he needs?

or would I rip him out of the driver's seat
and bring him to a dark basement room
like he might do?

the horror movie in my mind plays
toenails, pliers, swollen flesh
there is begging and screaming
chainsaws

as the birds chirp spring magic
and as the sun shines happy
I adjust the cord with the flick of my wrist
of my electric lawnmower
and continue to cut the grass of my suburban lawn
and I make sure my kids
are nearby
are away from the road
and as my imagination crawls out of its pit
I wonder who really is
the sick bastard?

Fashion Trend

Rice is the new pasta
       day jobs are the new slavery
              and suicide is the new cancer

Martha Stewart got
       five months
              for lying
                     (what's a couple hundred thousand?)

       and another reality TV show

a black man got
       shot
              for stealing a TV in ankle deep water
       down in New Orleans

the supermodels throw up
       and the cops yell "Throw down!"
              and somebody gets a tattoo
                    of a birthmark
                    on their ass

you order a beer
and it comes with a collectable mug
       and a coupon for liposuction

you take a shit
and read the poetry
       printed on the delicate tissue

you read this
and wipe
your
ass.

Helping Out

Check of the box
fill out the form

how are you going to make a difference?

buy a goat for a village
buy an outhouse too
free a child from sex slavery
vaccinate against poverty
recycle imagination
and kiss a communist

do it right away
do it online
do it for the children

read the review
try the new pastry
the one with chicken
and savory
at the charity
bake-off-tax-deduction sale
   (clean your plate and stuff your gob
    for the starving kids
     of Africa)

get all the rock musicians
to rub themselves down
with groupies
and platinum perfume
     record it
         and sell it on Blu Ray
    so we can all smoke hash
        and drool in 3-D
    so they can make a bundle
      but don't worry
         all the money goes to
   cancer monkeys
   and assisted suicide watchdogs

where is my yoga mat?
where is my Red Cross receipt?
where is my button that says, "I gave?"

we should all be feeling
    much better soon

don't worry
I made a donation
   I made a difference.

DAYDREAMING

a volcano lies within me
arm spread wide
as the surreal red ants
pour from my palms
crucified hands
            I sneak around
            like a thief
                    in the eternal Vegas night light
                    collecting images
            of the tacky
and now I've got my rhinestone suit
and I'm doing the Tarantino shuffle
and I've got poodles
and S+M slaves
            all on leashes
and we're going down the red carpet
and the cameras are flashing
and the fusion jazz is playing
and then . . .
            and then my wife
                    walks into the room
                            and asks
                            "What's Molly doing?"
            I look over at my daughter
                    – 2 months old –
                    and answer
                            "Sleeping."

Favourite Numbers

1. the winning numbers
   of your lottery ticket

2. the absence of numbers
   on your tombstone

3. the number of pi s
   hungry mathematicians can eat

4. the lipstick number of the waitress
   on a cocktail napkin

5. the number of friends
   you can count on

6. the numbers on the alarm clock
   before you throw it out the window

7. the number of times
   you lost track of counting

8. the number picked
   between one and ten

9. the numbers on the license plate
   before they drive off the cliff

10. the number of times
    you made love

11. the number of loves
    killed by time

12. the numbers
    of forgotten combination locks

13. the numbers that accidentally show up
    in your Alphagetti

14. the number 14
    just for good luck.

INTERCONNECTIVITY

The look on her face
– ah shit
from the drooling lips of a hot-dog bun
very yellow mustard falls
on a very new suit
and you watch this
as you drive by
on your dependable bicycle
while the look on his face
– oh shit
is observed by the intended recipient
of the Frisbee
which narrowly misses your head
and it UFO crashes
beside a couple
who are polluting the park with flesh
and coconut oil
and all of this is being scrutinized
by a young boy
with his grandfather's old telescope
from a distant balcony
and on the railing
there is an inch-worm
that is inching along
who becomes dinner
for brother blue-jay
and he soars high into the air
J. Livingston Seagull style
over the park
and the look on your face
– is that really bird shit?
as a white paste
dribbles down your face.

How Does Your Garden Grow?

I made an appointment
for a physical

I hadn't been in years

I had to wait a month
to be seen

two weeks in
I started having chest pains
panic attacks
I was full of meningitis
I was full of cancer
my heart was going
to give out
my spleen was about to burst
a stroke at any second

finally I got to see the doctor
and explained all this
to him

he told me he was glad
that I could recognize
the connection
between making the appointment
and coming down with
every serious disease possible

he told me my behaviour
was completely normal
that even he thought
from time to time
on the way home
"What am I growing today?"

then he fondled my testicles
and showed me how to look
for lumps

when I left the clinic
I felt much better
anxiety gone
cancer gone
heart murmurs
gone
just a sore shoulder
from a tetanus shot

I still had to do
the blood tests

the doctor told me it took
a week for the results
to come back

in that time
my imagination could grow
a tumour the size of a grapefruit

and in the shower the next day
I squeezed my balls
and asked myself
"What am I growing today?"

ODD DAY

Got up late
on the day of the dead
and played chess
with a mime

went for a walk
to the surrealist cemetery
and placed two fried eggs
on Dali's headstone

a crowd of zombies
watched old movies
projected on hot walls
of the mausoleum

walked further south
and found solace
on the menu
of the quick-fix diner
        (ordered spaghetti
                and meatballs instead)

walked home
and hung up
my shadow
for the night

plunked down
on the couch
with a drink
and watched
horrible sadness
on the news

brushed my teeth
and went to bed
and vowed
to get up
early.

ALL OF IT

The man who wins
despite the odds
and the assholes

the woman who kills
her abusive husband
with the bacon frying pan

the child who stands
and cries about his fallen ball
of chocolate ice-cream

the old man who stands
and cries about his fallen teeth
in the toilet

the maggot that eats
the infection off the face
of the car crash victim

the deerfly that eats
the bull-moose
on a sunny afternoon

the cute girl with the long legs
that go all the way
to Vancouver

the ugly dwarf
who eats peanut butter
and shoots smack

all of it
all of it will still be here
hurtling through space
when I'm long gone.

MOVING PAST – A PRAYER FOR CHRISTOPHER PAUCHAY

Yellow Quill Reserve
Saskatchewan
-50 Celsius outside
he dropped one
then the other
   (could he hear the screaming
   over the wind
     over the booze?)
then he collapsed
   exhausted – mind erased

eight hours later
he awakens in the hospital
through the haze of
hypothermia
whiskey
and asks, "Where are my kids?"

my wife cried
and told me
that this is why people
   need God
   to get past these things
   to move past these things

flipping through the paper
the next day
I see the Christmas photograph
of the happy family
   the girls
   just one and three
   only a half year difference
   between my own kids

just a diaper and a t-shirt
on each
        hopefully they didn't suffer too long out there
        in the snow

this is why
I can never believe
in God
and I pray that Christopher Pauchay
is not like me.

Monkey Magnet

I have a monkey
the Reese's Pieces kind
she likes to get into our bed
in the middle of the night

I usually vacate
end up in the basement
sleeping in the guest room

but this time my wife went
and the monkey got real close
she was too hot
on this summer night
I slid over
and she came along
like a fridge magnet

I ended up on the edge just   about   to fall o
                                                        ff
I got out and went around to the other side
to big open expanse of bed
then reverse polarity occurred
and she came scooting back across
and she mumbled
Can we watch that movie with Dorothy in it when we get
up?
The Wizard of Oz?
Yeah she said
Yeah I said
she went back to sleep
and I thought about following
the yellow brick road
and I thought about

a crow landing on my shoulder
a crow taking me into deep sleep
a crow leading me to Oz

I awoke to him cawing at my window
and a monkey drooling on my pillow.

Eclipse

The sun has forgotten
where I live

I grab extension cords
and lamps
and decorate the front lawn
with furniture flares
with light beacons

hey Mr. Sun
        I'm living down here
            see me?

I wake up on my couch
at noon
a racoon sits on the armrest
chewing a rotten apple core

my neighbour is
across the street
mowing his lawn
in his shorts
I wave
but I don't think he can see me
        it's too dark

I trip on a wire
        going inside

I shower and ready myself
for the day
but the day never comes

the sun has forgotten
where I live.

GUNSLINGER

I was walking
through Zellers
on my lunch hour
when I saw
a man
wearing a black
cowboy hat
and a long
black coat
heading towards
women's lingerie

I thought of
Clint Eastwood
and Lee Van Cleef

I thought
there is a possibility
of another man
wearing white
coming from
children's wear

I thought
newspaper headline
"Shooting at the Mall!"

then I was distracted
            toilet paper on sale
                  $4.99

there were no shots fired
just the clerk
who was late for his shift
for the last time.

EROSION

Carving my initials
in the ether
like the cart wheeling arms
of the skydiver
trying to grab at something
and only getting
handfuls of air

I know
it's all going
to be gone
one day
and hoping
for Nietzsche's eternal return
is just silly
            shit, you might as well
                    find religion

still
I can't help myself
and I continue
to write it
all down
anyway.

DYING HEALTHY

Life, the only game
in town it seems

I gave up smoking
so I could live
a little longer
long enough to watch
my babies
grow into children

I started jogging
so I could watch
my children
grow into adults

I gave up bacon
                    sausage
                              red meat
so I could meet
my grandchildren

I fear I will die
clutching a mixed green salad
with a strawberry vinaigrette dressing
and my grandson will say
at my funeral,
          "What a boring old fucker he was."

THE MOTH

I awake
in the middle
of the night
and I see it
on the dresser
resting

it's my manuscript
the top few pages
curling
up and down
breathing

I sit up in bed
and slowly
and carefully
roll up a magazine
off the nightstand

I slip out
of the covers

it sees me coming
and flies
into the air
pages fluttering wildly
jerking spastically
moth like
around the room
around my head

I swing at it

miss

"Piece of shit!" I scream

it flips
and flaps
and flies out the door
and down the hallway
and lands on the couch
in the living room

I grab a tennis racket
from the closet

it sees me coming
but this time
I'm too fast
and I wallop it
in mid flight
and it explodes
and the pages
scatter and fall
like snow globe snow
and a moment later
my wife walks in
and asks, "What are you doing?"

I answer her
          "Editing."

Old Friends

Cinderella's foot in a glass slipper
sometimes old friends fit right
        ten minutes
        ten months
        ten years
                time-travelers don't care

other friends
cast vampire shadows
over the things that never surface
over the doors that never get opened

and nervous eyes clock-watch
waiting for midnight
waiting for lies to turn into pumpkins
        when the intellectual carving knives come out

Halloween is upon us
        everyone carving wicked faces

these friends want candy niceties
        about the coolest fairy tale they just read
or they want your heart ripped out
        and given to them on a silver dish

these friends seem to get lost
        when they try to navigate through time.

Peach Cobbler

For the man
on the window ledge
I wish I could
present him
with the peach cobbler
and the black coffee
I had the other day

psychologists
            psychiatrists
                        the lady who is going to talk you
                                                d
                                                o
                                                w
                                                n

I say forget it
get the baker
            up there
                        with the espresso machine
give the man
            something to
                        live for.

Plastic Life

Lost in commemorative keychains
and the limited edition collector's cup
of this instant life
        (just add water
                AA batteries
                        and therapy)

we can make it through
another day
while somebody else
works hard
        (I like to piss into a clean toilet)

shove vitamin pills
into every orifice
and dance happy
along the religious sidewalk sales
        (zealots get a discount on explosives)

this is where the post-modern
capitalist dream
turns into the surrealist nightmare
where the woman on the billboard
is about to moan in orgasmic pleasure
if you would just pull out your plastic card
if you would just buy it
if you would just eat it
if you would just
        do it
she would shoot
dollar signs
out her pussy
and you would

be enlightened
to a discount
on your next
reincarnation.

POETRY

You find it
in the oddest
of places
>   funerals
>   bars
>   inside expired milk jugs

sometimes you turn
over a rock
and it crawls out
and slimes onto your shoe

other times you look
and look
and all you can see
is the blinking cursor
on your computer screen

and sometimes
BAM!
it comes out of nowhere
and hits you so hard
that it rattles your karma cage
that it rattles your bones

it can change your
rose coloured
eyeball prescription

it can change
the world.

A Clean Shave

I shaved the face off of my poem
and the words landed at the bottom
of the page
black little pieces of letter stubble
looking like bits of salt licorice
looking like extinguished candle wicks
looking like metal shavings
looking like the exclamation points from a conversation
        where people were screaming
looking like an orgy of ants
looking like the drawings of Jean Cocteau in a blender
looking like the jumbled musical notes from a Paganini
        composition
looking like a foreign language
looking like cigar ash
looking like miniature footprints for Sherlock Holmes
        to follow
looking like the lead tips of broken pencils
looking like the eyes of sharks
looking like a smashed pair of Buddy Holly's glasses
looking like a small section of a starry night sky
looking like the fingernails of coal miners
looking like the feathers of crows

I threw aftershave on my poem
and all the words ran together like an angry mob
and I turned my poem into a Rorschach ink-blob
and I couldn't see
anything in it
anymore.

Post Christmas in the Cubicle

I can hear whisperings
snippets of dialogue
from one of my colleagues
on the other side
of my cubicle wall
recounting his Christmas vacation

a lot of food, a *lot* of food

then driving, then more food

then more driving, then more food

then shovelling

food

driving to Aylmer
driving to Gatineau

two tables set up with food

we only get it once a year

tourtiere, different kinds of meat, desserts

"I'm glad it's over," he said

I have a vision of my colleague
exploding like that guy
in "The Meaning of Life"
my ceiling tiles covered in
tourtiere, different kinds of meat, desserts

after his story ends
I hear the soft sounds
of keyboards popping away
like microwavable popcorn

the air vent above me rattles and hisses
like dissolving Alka-Seltzer tablets.

Fuck Religion

Her ass was
Jesus Christ

her tits were
salvation

every night
my cock
would stand up
and say
the Lord's Prayer

then one day
she upped and left me

my liver
began to see
stars

I dreamed
about pushing priests
down elevator shafts

I lost my faith

but then I found
a nice girl
with an atheist pussy

and she would
still scream
"Oh God!"
when she came.

PUKE

The pop culture factories
are pumping out
the latest
organic plastic injectable
and the fastest snortable underwear
and the most downloadable multimedia fascists

here come the sex dolls that scream political rhetoric
and shoot ice cream from their tits

here comes the day job that you can't quit
because your wallet has been hooked
on violent bubblegum puke

here comes the foreign five minute
not-too-spicy cultural noodle experience

here comes the commemorative special anniversary
limited edition stainless steel shoehorn

the cream-pie wars have started
        (30 minutes at 350)
        and the terrorists target Mr. Microphone
            and the Sound Byte Gang

and we are all going to feel the pinch of cholesterol
as the cowboy rides the disco-ball
into the sunset
        the clown falls into a diabetic coma
                and the credits cinnamon-roll off the screen

that's the puke
lick it up.

Eggtimer

Sat on a three minute egg
for an anxious hour
hatched a synthetic monster
which farted apparitions
of grain fed chickens

gave birth to a cheeseburger
got hormones spinally injected
stripped of medals
found mayonnaise in my urine

stuffed dead chickens into bowls
of brown sauce wine
coupons expired
while waiting in line

no time left
got it to go.

Waiting for the Words

When you creep
into the night
sometimes the words
hide

you spit and scream
and make threats to the air
but the words stay
hidden

sometimes the words
come easy
if you don't force them
out of their holes
with bags of magic

when they come out
on their own
they dance around
the page
like a young couple
in love

tonight you drink
to let them out
then the whole bottle
is empty
and still the words stay
hidden

so you wait
and wait
but nothing comes.

Work the Cliché

Work the cliché
fold it into itself
pull its head out
through its ass
flip it
make it dance
dress it up in scuba gear

work the cliché
like a dog
like a slum landlord
works his tenant

work the cliché
beat it out
beat it down
beat it sideways
beat it senseless
beat the shit out of it

work the cliché
work it until
        it has suffered
        like Jesus on the cross
work it until
        it cries for its mamma
work it until
        you taste blood
work it until
        it's reborn

then it will give off the smell of originality
the scent of genius
the ripe stench of
"I wish I had written that"
yes, work the cliché
then work it again
then you will walk with medals
and trophies
people will pat you on the back
buy you a drink
pop a cigar into your mouth
and send you to bed with an overinflated ego.

Rock Star Poet

I am the rock star poet
jet setting around the globe
giving readings
with my lighting crew
and my make-up people
and my wardrobe consultants
and my poet groupies
and my own private chef
and my manager
and my chauffeur

when I drink my champagne
and orange juice
in the mornings
while somebody
works on my hair
and nails
I worry

not about the daily press conferences
or the stress of fame
or what to do with all my money
no, none of that

I worry about deeper issues

that's because I'm
a sensitive artist
a sensitive poet
a sensitive rock star
poet

I worry
that there won't be enough
oxygen
to sustain the globe
because
they keep cutting
and cutting
and cutting
all the trees down
to print more and more
and more
volumes
of all my writings

but this is the high price
of art
I guess

and I must bear this burden
I must bear it
alone.

Your Name

Yes you have the greatest hits collection
yes you have the facebook account
yes you have the starring role
you are the headliner

you get on the label
you get on the cover
you get on the bandwagon

so you get your name on the T-Shirt
so you get your name on the billboard
so you get your name on the door
so you get your name on the dinner invite
so you get your name on the trophy
so you get your name on the medal·
so you get your name on the platinum credit card
so you get your name up in lights

but finally
you get your name
on
the headstone

maybe they will name
a street after you
So-and-so Parkway
Jane-Doe Street

maybe they will erect
a statue
so the drunks
can piss on your name

maybe.

So Clever

as creatures
we haven't been
around
all that long
but that human brain
wow
two and a half
thousand years
since Thales
and
      we have robots on Mars

claws
teeth
muscle
      they got nothing
on the human brain

science
      mathematics
           imagination

Maybe a few hundred years more
and we'll kill ourselves off?

      and do you know what is funny about this?
claws teeth and muscle
      they don't see the humour in it
they don't see the humour
in anything.

Sunday Meditation

Your brain keeps pumping out
        the existential rhythm and blues
                identity is an illusion
                there is no you
                just being

determinism dances its
        forceful tap
                on the inside of your
                        skull

do you have a choice to think otherwise?
        can you dance to the tune
                of a different set of neurons?

then contemplation
        is destroyed by
                        DING-DONG

(wasn't it always going to happen this way?)

somebody at the front door
        a kid selling leaf bags for charity

you tell him "It must be fate"

he looks at you a little bewildered
        a little afraid

you ask him "How much?"
        he says "$5 for four bags"

you fish into your pocket and give him the money
      he says "Thanks" and gives you the bags and walks away

you think, one day the human race will be gone
you think, one day it will all be gone
you think, identity may be illusion, but it's all you have for
now
you think, the community hockey league is $5 richer

you watch a yellow leaf fall

you think, you should rake the front yard.

THE THING WITH BUKOWSKI IS

You have to follow him
around the race track
then drive mad with him
down the freeway
then go home with him
to the beer empties
and the ashtrays
and the whores
and the fights
and the fan-mail
and the cats
and the bathtub
and the Bee
and the beer shits
and the solitude
and all the goddamn
rest of it

and you read this
over and over
and over

but then WHAM!
       he hits you with a line
       that opens a smile wide
       on your tin can face
       and you think
       shit, I wish
       I had written that.

Packaged Thighs for Irving Layton

At 35000 feet
I watched this woman
with packaged thighs
wait for the bathroom

I was reading Irving Layton
and the woman across the aisle
was reading Danielle Steele
but out of the corner
of my wandering eye
I could see those packaged thighs
moving like a prancing horse
about to break into a gallop
with the anticipation
of sweet urination
or the sexual movement
before climatic release

and all I wanted to do
was check out her ass
to see if it matched
those muscular packaged thighs

and to my horror
an obvious blob of a man
oblivious to the packaged thighs
obscured my chance of a view
by standing next in line
the bastard
just like a TV transmission
cutting out on your last
winning lottery ticket number:
I couldn't see

she went in
she came out

but divine intervention
came in the form
of a seat number
less than mine

she bent over
to get something
by her seat
and that's when I saw
her ass was flat.

NOT YET

When I heard
that Michael Crichton died
at age 66
from cancer
the next morning
I lay in bed
and pictured myself
lying in a hospital
floating in the air
like in "Coma"
tubes running out of me
wires sticking in me
keeping me alive

as I imagined this
science-fiction nightmare
I could hear the cawing
of the crows
flying by
outside my window

it was time to
get up
get dressed
and get to work

science has not yet
figured out
how to turn off
the aging gene

until then
we are left with
just fiction

and that day
I flew to work.

FOR THE HOPE OF ONE MORE DAY

I'm moving down the street
in my sneakers
       panting
iPod drowning out my own
heartbeat
      footsteps
           panting

the trees have all been cut
into the shapes of ice-cream scoops
or fuzzy green chairs from the seventies
to accommodate wires

I think about my father
women, cigarettes, and art
did it for him

but above all, food
he would smother
everything down in gravy
and smoke a coffin nail after

he died from pancreatic cancer

I think about my stepfather
women, cigarettes, and words
did it for him

but above all, booze
a bottle of red with dinner
then off to the pub
for pints and darts and talk
of Hemingway

I think about sitting with him
in the pub, drinking
blowing smoke until the air
was dolphin blue

he died from bladder cancer

I think about my father-in-law
booze, cigarettes, and history
did it for him
but above all antiques
years spent in Ontario barns
filled with old bottles
and rusted wagon wheels
looking for treasures

he changed his life around
found AA
found Jesus
found a personal trainer

and he was just walking
staying healthy
when he died from a heart attack

there are no guarantees
that putting in my miles
eating squirrel food
will do any good
but I think about my kids
school plays
that I have not yet attended
ceremonies
that I have not yet witnessed

booze, cigarettes, women, words
food, movies, sunsets, art
breathing and the spaces
in between
it all does it for me

but above all my family

so I put in my miles
always for the hope
            of one more day.

MAINLINING

I used an old rusty
         fountain pen

to shoot a poem
         into my arm

I began to
         piss butterflies

and I fell down
                  down

                           down
and when I hit the floor
         I threw up stanza
                  after stanza
                           of flowery rainbow words

I managed to pull it together
I staggered down the street
and fell into a store
and bought a black beret
and turtleneck
and smoked a pack of cigarettes
and drank a million cups of coffee
and finally I was coming down
         off my poem

when I ran into my dealer

tucked under his arm
         like a preacher man carrying a bible
         he had
"In the Clear: A Contemporary Canadian Poetry Anthology"

he ripped out a page like a doctor tearing off a script
    "Try this, it will blow your mind"
    "No thanks," I said "I'll stick with prose"

I went home
and chugged back some Hemingway
and chased it down with a little Steinbeck
and watched my hand
stop shaking.

MOTIVATION

Jesus put a gun to my head
and said
        "Write mother fucker"

and so I did
and my hand shook
and I explained I didn't want to die
and he said "Shut up and write"
and I began the poem of my life
and metaphors the size of the sun
        tumbled out of me
                like drunks out of the bar
and similes of genius were like everywhere
and the onomatopoeia was tickety tickety boo
and the alliteration was well what we would wail,
"Wonderful!"
and Jesus smirked when I was done

smirked while he read what I had written
smirked while I was squirming in my chair
smirked while the sweat was pouring off of me
smirked while I was wondering if I was going to die

he said, "there you go"
he said, "every poem should be this good,
        you just need to be motivated."

and off he went
whistling
that gun toting sandaled mother fucker

he taught me
to keep the faith.

Personal

We don't talk
anymore

we just speak
in small circles
with eggshell voices
about the weather

we used to talk loud
walk through walls

we dove on grenades
and off of cliffs

we don't talk
anymore

we just speak.

Playing Dress Up

My right arm extends out
        muscle in the forearm tight
            red nylon twirling like candy cane
               to the end
                    where a basset hound is pulling
                     front legs
                       paws and nails dragging me
                              to smell
                              another
                              dog's piss

my left arm
is holding
my six year old
daughter's leg
who's
resting high
on my
shoulders

at night we go out to dinner
and she asks me
if she can wear her fairy costume
with butterfly wings
"Of course" I tell her

soon she will be too big
to carry on my shoulders
and she will not want to wear
costumes out to dinner

at this
I grow a little sad

after dinner
we visit the hippie shop next door
and I purchase the stupidest
looking straw cowboy hat
you ever did see

"Good day, Madame" I say
tipping my hat to the cashier

at this
she smiles

at this
I grow a little happy.

SNAPSHOT

The poems I write
are sometimes
a snapshot of an emotion
or a moment in time
like the photograph you took
with your mind
of your father's distorted face
as he screamed at your mother

the poems I write
are sometimes
written at your expense
because I robbed
our friendship's unspoken words
like an orphan robbing
your family photographs
and pretending they're his own

the poems I write
are sometimes vain
because of my own need
for glimmering glory
and pedantic praise
like the greed of a child
waiting to collect
the last baseball-card
to complete his set
and show up his friends

the poems I write
are sometimes beautiful
when they capture
a youthful moment
like your eye
catching a glimpse
of your girlfriend's bosom
down her open top
as you move to kiss her
on a warm sunny summer day

the poems I write
are sometimes all of these
and sometimes none
but I continue
to snap and click
at my keyboard
and wait for the good shot
to develop
like a coach waiting
for his boxer
to develop a good left jab.

SOME ADVICE

Crying
that you haven't
written a poem
in three months
after the way
you treated the cashier
at the deli
makes me
angry and embarrassed

write from the gut
and be nice
to people
who make
your sandwich
your fuel
for
your gut

these are not little people
these are people
and maybe you should
sign up
for some life lessons
because these people
make your sandwich
not out of joy
not out of love for you
but because they
need to

you
should write
poems
for the same reason.

The Splash of 'hello'

my time suffocated
by a ringing phone

and I
a small child
at the edge of a dock
about to jump
into a still black lake
not knowing
what tentacles
and teeth
and slime
await me

sad souls
or somebody
wanting to sell me
credit card insurance
potentially wait
on the other end

and once
I let go
when toes uncurl
from the edge
of that wooden stability
which is grandpa's dock
there is no turning back

the splash of 'hello'
and seconds later
I am swimming
in conversation
about all the time
which has gone away
like water
down a sink

and somehow I
get back to dry land
and move
to a different room
only to hear
the sound
of waves again

it isn't near by
so I don't get it.

Theoretical Fear

Waiting for my turn to speak
and his voice fades out

and my ears turn hot
and my mouth turns dry
and people are clapping
and now someone is introducing
me

half way through
I realize
I'm going to make it
and then
people are clapping again
for
me

now I reclaim my seat
and my friends smile
to tell
me
I did a good job
and the guy
in front of
me
is scribbling
in a note pad
and I think journalist
but
he is drawing
little squares and circles
of
theoretical football plays.

VELOCITY ZERO

I heard on the news
after it was over
there were twice
as many people
because of the Queen

we were near the Terry Fox statue
a small square overlooking
the Parliament buildings

I saw a white speck in the distance
it was the Queen's hat

after alternating my children
on my shoulders
for half an hour
like carousel riders
it was time to go

we tried cutting through
the building behind us
but found ourselves trapped
in a tunnel of people
with the same idea

headlines flashed through my mind
      "Hundreds Injured in Stampede"
      "Canada Day Turns Tragic"
claustrophobia squeezed my heart – must get out of here
we made our way back to the square
we made our way back outside
                        air
me wearing a Canadian Flag like a cape

my four year old son again on my shoulders
we moved towards the sidewalk
we bunched up chest to back backtochesttightandthentighter
suddenly I was aware of a man screaming from a light post
at first I thought he might be drunk and calling out to his
       friends in the crowd
but then I saw the terror on his face
he had lost his little girl in this sea of red and white giant
       adults   gone
there was nothing I could do even though I was dressed like
       a superhero
I looked ahead and made sure my wife still had my daughter's
       hand
she looked scared
the man on the light post continued to scream his little girl's
       name
ten minutes passed and I'd traversed only a foot
finally cops show up and somebody yelled to the man
that they think she is inside the building behind him
he thanked them but couldn't go anywhere
there was no place to go
and he continued to scream
and he continued to scan the crowd
and I held on to my son's legs
and waited to move
and watched my wife and daughter
disappear around a corner
right before my eyes.

Writing for the People

What I want to know
is why there is so much
bad writing kicking around
like parking meters
or sad shoes
the shit seems to be everywhere

and the people's poetry
has moved from Grossman's blues bar
to Chapters' coffee bar

nobody even blinked an eye
while corporate thugs
with faces like meatloaf
and red rat eyes
kicked the living snot out of Milton Acorn
in a dirty side alley

Milt
lying crumpled
and pissed on
and bruised
and stinking
saw old Bukowski crawl out
from a fly infested dumpster
with a fifth of whiskey
and sit down across the alley

"the revolution is for shit Milt
the people are for shit
and do you know
who has the best selection of my poetry?
and maybe yours too? Chapters.
care for a drink?"

and as the camera pulls back and away
from these two caricatures sitting in an alley
sharing a bottle
we cut to me
sitting here
writing this

I'm pushing against the odds.

Venn Diagram

The intersection
       of a woman
walking three small dogs
on three leashes

      and

          two traffic poles

   =

         a book of sailing knots
            performed by a contortionist
     wearing fuzzy slippers

 my laughter was logical

then I found the angles

and   helped   her   get   free.

TRYING TO

She came in
while I was trying to take
a nap

she said "You should be writing"

I said "I wrote a poem"

she said "I don't like your poems"

she said "Slice of life, who cares?"

I didn't say anything
I just waited until she left
then wrote it
down.

Wart War I

I had an unexpected foe
move into the basement
of my big toe

that's when the war
started

I took the scissors to him
and hacked at him
like a butcher
handling cheap meat

this went on for
months

he would retreat a bit
then advance
when I got lazy

I even tried biting
the little bastard off
(my foot in my mouth
common for me)

there was pain
and screaming
and cursing
and torture

War is HELL!

then I got nasty
Chemical Warfare
Compound W

but he held out
like a rebel army
in the flesh forest
of my calloused skin

so I went at him
with both guns BLAZING

then it was all over
I had won
victory was mine
I had regained the toe

but you know
to this day
I still miss the fight.

You carry it with you

You carry it with you
like a rat
that is forever chewing
on your heart

you carry it with you
like a pallbearer
this lust for life
this desire to push beyond
just a day job
and a can of soup

you carry it with you
these hopes
and dreams
of literary touchdowns
of gold medal words
printed in the thousands
of books that keep
flying off the shelves

you carry it with you
like a ball of wet clay
in your gut
this feeling that you
could win the race

you carry it with you
and sometimes it makes you cry
and sometimes it makes you insane
and sometimes it does nothing
but piss you off

but you still carry it with you
just the same.

THROUGH THE FROST

Shovelling wet snow
hunky bits
that look like cheese curds

garlic skin angels fly
from my mouth
and disappear
in the early morning
winter air

my children bang at the window
to let me know
they are watching
that they are there

I think of photographs
like they had been washed
in lemon and milk
       my father
       shovelling our driveway
       in the 1970s
       snow banks the size of
       polar bears

me in 2008
we could be twins
lost in time

I write this down for them
a photograph of reasons
so they will know
I was watching too.

Sea Monster

The days come at you
like a slow moving
sea monster

Monday always screams
          like Janet Leigh

Roger Corman is Tuesday

Wednesday is snowing so hard
that the house across the street
looks like it has bad reception

Thursday is the last breath
before being dragged under

Friday is the stake through the heart

after an attack
          day job cuts
          and bruises cover
          your soul
you swallow the bag
of I.V. meds
          a belly full of beer
                              whiskey
                    salty won ton soup

keep yourself sedated
                    hydrated
                    healing.

Big Bird Dream

Frozen in time
wasting away
waiting
for it to happen

letting go of the dream
is as easy as
a crazy-glue truck
smashing into a pillow factory

so now you look like
a chicken

and who wants
to represent a chicken?

if they could only see
you're not trying to fly
you're waving
"Hey, over here!"

you sigh
go home and try
to shit out a golden egg
and you remember you're not
a goose
but just a man with quills.

The Gentle Sleeper

You have finally gotten
her down
and you lie there
in bed
you and your wife
like you were lying on
very thin ice
afraid to move
afraid to hear
a new tooth
cracking the surface
a howl that could shatter
and plunge you both into
the cold waters
of a sleepless night

A WHIMPER

we clutch our pillows
              like lifejackets

SILENCE

wait
        wait
                wait

SILENCE

we hold our breath
and slowly crawl
towards shore
towards sleep.

THE RIDE

Locked into this
a mad clock
that spins
with endless time
and we surf
      but the second hand

the big picture can't save you

you whiz by
on this existential exhibition ride
and the carnie
who looks like Jesus
asks, "Do you want to go faster?"

some days it's hard
to face the face
you forget to live in the moment
distracted by the ticking
      sounds like nuts and bolts
          falling off the machinery

when the ride stops
stomach a little queasy
you dig frantically in your pocket
for more tickets
but the clowns come
and walk you to the big gate.

IDENTITY

like an ugly scarf
that you received as a gift
and feel obliged to wear

wear the dad hat
wear the missionary love making birthday suit
wear the dog collar for the full on sexcapades
wear the wacky co-worker joy buzzer
wear the kid gloves
wear the shoulder pads to cry on
wear the poetry pants
wear the Mr. Green Jeans of the friendly neighbour

if you are given a gun and camouflage
does that make you a soldier?
does that make you a willing participant?
does that make you the enemy?

the tickle trunk of imagination
Norman Bates dressed up as his mom
serial killers dressed up like clowns
George W. Bush dressed up like the president

a caterpillar
wrapped up in the cocoon
of Wittgenstein's family resemblance
there emerges a butterfly
a thousand shades of blue and brown

I think therefore I am what?
just thinking?
maybe no more special
than a muscle flexing?

you adjust yourself in the mirror
and walk out into the world
and pretend to be
yourself
and you accept it
like you accept breathing.

REMINDER

The days stretch out
like a prison sentence

the other night I dreamt
about a family
Christmas party
and a crow
had gotten stuck
inside the house
flapping about
crashing into things
squawking away

I had to try
and shoo him out

was he a reminder
          of death?
was he a reminder
          of a day job?
maybe the same thing?

I managed to
get him out
but he stood outside
the window
and watched me
sip my eggnog

little fucker.

LIFE SENTENCE

What is this thing?

10, 20, 50, maybe even a 100 years? months? days? seconds?
stillborn?

and what do you do with the time?

what are you going to be when you grow up?

counter culture revolutionary, tax collector, bomb dropper,
grave digger, software engineer, poet, ostrich farmer, chess
master
computer results from the High School Career Aptitude Test

board games
a lifetime of farts
pancakes on Sunday mornings
cleaning out the garage
online shopping

so you read philosophy books
so you join a cult
so you do yoga
so you do hash
so you do what comes naturally

you get a degree
you get a refund
you get a parking ticket
you get the special of the day
you get a pension
you get laid

you buy a hotdog
you buy life insurance
you buy a get-well card
you buy a shiny new plasma electroencephalogram
you buy it hook, line and sinker

you work on your stamp collection
you work on your novel
you work on your day off
you work on your Zen garden
your work on your control issues

do you ride it all the way to the last stop? cancer, heart
attack, stroke
     or do you get off early? pills, rope, shotgun

god left the building with all his friends
and what are you left with?
     popsicle sticks and glue and a bucket of self motivation

what are you going to be when you grow up?

what is this thing?

what are you going to do with all the time?

ACKNOWLEDGEMENTS

Some of the poems in this collection have previously appeared (in some form) in the following publications: *Bywords*, *Ottawater*, *ditch*, *Misunderstandings*, *The Moose and the Pussy*, *All Rights Reserved*, *On Spec*, *Leaf Press—Monday's Poem*, *Raven Poetry: Online Poetry Journal*, and *The Writers Block*.

I would like to thank all my friends and family for the constant love and support. I would like to mention a few names that I just couldn't forget (wink!): Jessica Chinn, Andrina Cox, Bobbi Jo Bradley, Gordon Puddister, Samantha Tattersall, Rita and Gerald Haakman, Reid Doig, Alexander Hannay, Jocelyne Payeur, Shahriar Hoque, Joanne Lee, Steve Turner, Joanne Wright-Hicks, Jason Holbrough, Dan and Abi Roberts, and Sandy and Brenda McPherson.

To new friends: Lisa Gregoire and Dan Rubinstein, Patrick and Kristy Donnelly, Hassan Alikhan, Jeffery Clarke, Sophie Hargest, Andrew Drew Lahaise, Dale Dalessio, Heather Sherman, Andrew Strome, Lauren Aldwinckle, Andrea Cats, and Lisa Mounteer.

Much gratitude to Michael Dennis, Jim Johnstone, Amanda Earl, Susan Johnston, and Chris Needham.

The elusive, ethereal, and very genuine Sidney Shapiro—thank you, sir.

And finally to Judith Gustafsson (my favourite photographer), my beautiful and wickedly smart wife Marty, my monkey Molly and my pal Henry—love you guys with all my heart.